red earth

by

by rob mclennan

© Copyright rob mclennan 2003

National Library of Canada Cataloguing in Publication

McLennan, Rob, 1970-
        Red earth / Rob McLennan.

(Palm poets series ; 05) Poems.
ISBN 0-88753-381-7

1. Prince Edward Island—Poetry. I. Title. II. Series.

PS8575.L4586R42 2003   C811'.54   C2003-902756-2
PR9199.3.M33413R42 2003

The Palm Poets Series is published by Black Moss Press at 2450 Byng Road, Windsor, Ontario N8W 3E8. Black Moss books are distributed in Canada and the U.S. by Firefly Books, 3680 Victoria Park Ave., Willowdale, Ont. Canada. All orders should be directed there.

Black Moss would like to acknowledge the generous support of the Canada Council and the Ontario Arts Council for its publishing program.

I am afraid
of this country of bones
this arid valley
> - *Cecelia Frey,*
> *the least you can do is sing*

by the same author:

paper hotel
harvest, a book of signifiers
bagne, or Criteria for Heaven
The Richard Brautigan Ahhhhhhhhhhh
Manitoba highway map
bury me deep in the green wood
Notes on drowning

editor

GROUNDSWELL, best of above/ground press, 1993-2003
evergreen: six new poets
side/lines: a new canadian poetics
YOU AND YOUR BRIGHT IDEAS: NEW MONTREAL WRITING
Shadowy Technicians: New Ottawa Poets
Written in the Skin

some of these pieces have appeared as *black box #1* (ON), *The Carleton Arts Review* (ON), in *dark leisure* (MB), *The Drunken Boat* (www.drunkenboat.com, Texas), in an issue of jwcurry's *news notes* (room 302 books, Ottawa), *The Night of the Living Instant Anthology* (Toronto Small Press Group, 2000), *Optimism Monthly* (Czech Republic), *Journal of Literature and Aesthetics* (India), as various above/ground press poetry broadsides & the chapbooks *red earth* (2002, above/ground press) & *voice over 1.0 + 1.5* (2002, camenae press) & broadcast on David Rimmington's The Poetry Show (CKDU, Dalhousie University Radio), Click Here (CHUO, University of Ottawa Radio) & on CFMU (McMaster University).

thanks to jwcurry, unbelievable friend & resource, who lent his apt for 3 months, that long summer of '00, where/when this book was given form. thanks, too, to Gil McElroy for, among other things, curating the bpNichol show in Charlottetown that same summer.

unofficial soundtrack by emm gryner.

red earth

for sandie drzewiecki

red earth (preface

i

all those words you didnt need to use
& then

wrappt up like a tongue around the sun
the axeman filling

aperture

& grace

ii

   (of gods & plastic demons

     /it doesnt matter where they fall
      there always
     is one
       (or why

suddenly thinking abt china & the wheel
& the length of the flight

  i need a place to go in dreamtime

   /what language

     internal/interval

  scope of cloud

red earth (one

i

      stayd in a hotel in cavendish
      across from green gables, anne

            a night, w/ an e

(wrote my name)

- suddenly (red earth

hurried to wait   minutes
bodies wrap joint
       cavendish

(log books, recording notation)

/shore north

      & shone

            (where mary jane

ii

        (this is not my land, its...

green green always green
brown walls motel one room
   two beds (wha
         tever

)irving gas

 & grows
growth of avonlea
& marilla, tourists who
  cant divide
     the fiction
    (colleen dewhearst

who reminded then of
mary jane, then
who reminded her
  of her mother, own

then

/the relationship of self

iii

japanese couple
        wedding dress
take pictures (silence

reverence) outside
annes house
(haunted woods

)keep hands

iv

interpretive forest (reading

scraps
       (what lucy maud wrote
(lost) said

   singing

(in woods, the)
              by the highway, couple gets
    hitched
      (married)

   music at work

 (red sand
    in all my pockets

earth & fire
              shoes

highway   refuels

(island small enough

v

somewhere to no   earth goes
      where

shoes & pockets   small circles

both

& payphone   change is coming
red car thick
     disappears
in small lots

vi

day one -

      highway fingers a blue
line going up & learning
scale of

thot   & postcards
of anne shirleys house
built from
its original run music
videos in the
      motel room flashing
lights & open
window   cant tell
anything abt any
one red

lobster

vii

day three -

      put back   up
          in a rental
apple blossoms &

            home
of the pumpkin people

         annapolis
& first permanent set

viii

green: gables, houses w/ red
        roofs, green gables, "the colour

    of spring", water from an angle (certain

red:
      earth, sand dunes
     & fingers, fissures run thru dry

                blood creek, what the mi'kmaq
                        might tell

      other ways (wise)   open wine
        in the back seat

    & eyes in the morning, sore
    & older

ix

1979
parents & i
driving three days down
from farm to cavendish - to the
same three stops
in carefree accident
of agenda - green
gables, wax
museum, car
& farm equipment museum,
to same age daughter
now & her at home,
waiting, her
turn

    - asks me later, if we
went to legoland
        , didnt know

water good against the bare skin
strait of _____

x

day (negative) two

        (sleeping halifax

a modest requiem
    beside the atlantic

   in montreal, 100,000 mourners
pay homage to the rocket

        john grisham novels
dont mean anything
    to polar bears

xi

live from red

rocks in sand

    (crumble

bridge effect & swings

take the ferry out

    (initial

nfl ferries & the

pilferd coffee mug

    (says so

at the close, she

wants to hear music

xii

(to reclaim the small gesture)

    h

            t

                a

              e

         r

      b

xiii

photograph memory,
    not photographic

red beach on the shore north,
piping plover nesting

(area closed)

walks a mile to the east
brush gate   (prohibitive

couch washes up on sand
rock/wood buffer
claims it

        (little nemo
         'neath dreamland
        waves

single lane passing

xiv

day four -

       rips violently apart,
what means, or thru
rain on the
          ground, or

sky, soil
makes a broth of
white set
sail

into the under
growth o'er
sea

XV

    foot on the ground, step

red shale red car red floor
back where
    sand map
of the backtrack

    imagines us, keeps

(will not stop raining

xvi

    the preliminary function of this
    a recording of _____

what says my hair or writes a
postcard, petshop in
charlottetown, see-thru
   fish, block
of brains & lungs, neon
flush, the eye thru
function, primarily
as tail, & skeleton
of

/editas eyes

      every phone call, not
the one i should be making,
home
      her,
not her,
she

xvii

day three (again) -

        in turbulent
oasis, first
a bedspread, first
a television set, home
again, first
the questions arise
returned, first
the gas tanks,
mileage, first
the wine still, first
the method of inquiry,
secrets & touch, first
& more than a simple

retelling

xviii

    - tale of mary jane

who ran away from north shore
home, at
fifteen, toronto
waitress, eventual
marriage, some
   children, number
six who found my
place & cofound
kate, three generations
   of women against
the telling, this
red land in their
blood, is
land is
    re(a)d
as island, here
a bridge, a
line, no
longer
is

red

voice-over 1.0

for jennifer mulligan

your socks on the floor that first night: a youness
 - Nicole Markotic, Minotaurs & other alphabets

you take away the frame / a vacuum
tearing off eyebrows

the convergence of fluids & body marks
nail scratches   small bruises

widen   small (   ) of the back

taken in that first time   when everything

History. Can we still draw on that obsolete authority?
- *Milan Kundera, Testaments Betrayed*

in the darkness of

pleasure & past previous lives interweave

moving thru the walls like air (

complicated wings full of blue shadows.
   - *Sharon Thesen, A Pair of Scissors*

what is impossible enough to document, or drive a wedge between.
goose wings enough to break an arm,
                              what chance

have others.   mythologies of angels
& small spirits, centred amid heart/break. what colours

do air, or the regions
of sleep. make your move. oil based, even

fast food milkshakes take the lit match.

I'm just emphasizing what we might have forgotten.
- Louis Dudek, Open Letter, series six, 2-3

depends what digit holds. depends where.

fingers in a love. watch hands slip over
& under, take
like a knife.

language as a grasp for air. the rain
       hits hard against the pavement.

cave paintings that exist in the now, never
the past, whether recent or ancient.

the berry juice
remains fresh.   expectations fail.

& nothing else comes up to the point you began.

What the Inquirer is trying to do, here, is allegorize
 - *Mark Cochrane, Dumbhead*

down to the lowest com, "she cant leave yet, im
    not out of condoms," trying out

for something deeper. not made. want to go to bed
at night. wonderful somehow, no matter

    & then breaks. a big open field. tears the
coffee filter in half. play fighting on the balcony, or
two headed kittens, & wolves.

i dont believe you when you say. who cares.
i havent a clue. takes a fork lift, crane
    & roof removal to get

the 400-pound corpse clear. the heart, too, tho its
    too vague. that by itself,

means nothing.

Philosophy is nothing more than god throwing his voice.
- Kevin Connolly, Pterodactyls

where we used to be. which one
    the speaker & which one spoke. from

the comfort of your mouth.

parts are speaking, speech. i mean
nothing to your knees.

i want to be the poet
of your elbows, every joint. back there
    when rain was what wed launch

into, not away. sugar made.
    from my back deck,
the neighbours could see everything. god

was hidden by the trees.

Slow foot, & swift foot, death delays but for a season.
 - *Ezra Pound, Selected Poems*

to find the meaning of the consecrated flesh

mary magdelaine, how unfairly maligned
    by so much christian scholarly

"gold & love affairs" - had my share,
    now soon again, the tarot tells

im on my way, the five of swords retorts,
    the world card, arcana major

& all four elements, facing out
    my hopes & fears, my final outcome

> **feet in the shifting surf   surface   of the word**
> *- bpNichol, The Martyrology Book 6, Hour 9*

holding fast to one thing, claws
on the hammer

for the meat of it, lungs   escapade

or escape   side of the
heart of the   one thing

mouth

erosion   a tearing down
of numbers   reduced to

in winter, when before me, cross my path

in summer, when behind me, cross my path
  - *Charles Olson, Selected Writings*

the steps & feet from solstice, summer
& sun haze painting thru the clouds
   at stonehenge templar moon

rising solar cross one against love
& barely exists part of the season

   of mists & days end

blankets wrappt around the legs held still
   from moving

Cloth is one thing. both have drifted, and speech unbuttons my thing.
   - Erin Moure

to wonder where the pigment faded. say the word
    & it becomes yours.

list everything you know of saints & sages,
    the phone numbers
of all those claims. divisive.

my view of somerset overlaps the bus routes,
tour groups that gape me
    pencilling the window. take one.

they always go the wrong lean on the hill.
push up, not down, & end up
    guzzling gas to get nowhere.

expansive figures lay.

while our innovations, instead, simply accumulate and add to the pos- / sibilities.
   - Dick Higgins

back into the fashion by the time (

) fixed gaze, however altered

on to the next already (

) when i could have been learning something

We no longer know / what dances bring the rain
  - Robert Hogg, Standing Back

brought back into the suggestiveness of mystery,

timelines & the ventriloquists stare, both hands
    are neither on the table.

the same story as the old one, the only one
    i know: the necessity
of birds, stars, chimneys, trees, etc.

you lean back into the hollow tree, what prince
    bestowed upon the royal oak?

look up on the sliding tides. not even
the fixed view means anything. scope,

or girders.

If I do not act, the worlds will perish.
   - *Krishna, The Bhagavad Gita*

a dance of subatomic particles, matter vs energy.

where considered, motion as the essential
        property, modern physics

& matter. does it matter. a certain movement

gets into her head to denote. gets into
        her head & wont come clean.

stop where we stand. pause effect
        that even bullets cant penetrate.

& what keeps alive, turning circles in the sun.

The din / of traffic is almost more bearable than the garden
   - Sue Sinclair

see where it gets you: giving birth.

an apology of stones is forthcoming. a treatise
        on the movement of weeds never comes.

two thousand pounds of hurtling steel
        & glass, to make out
in the back seat

at seventeen. whatever you drive.

tongue lasts longer than the skin. without
        the promises & guidelines of speech.

or borders of them. trapped in the frame.

You don't speak for me; you don't speak for anyone.
  - Emm Gryner, Science Fair

whatever i dream of you became musical.

the evolution of the step. white clouds
    turning rain just over the tree-line.

(   )

where english is the secondary. even third.

one perception must follow immediately and directly on a further perception
   - Robert Creeley

correspondence raging out of control. postcards
    & thank-you notes slide thru the slot.

how does the freedom explain the frame? how do
    firearms & flame-throwers really differ?

its one thing to hear the talking doll
    swear like a drunken sailor. gratuities
out of teddy ruxpin.

dont be putting words in my mouth.

popcorn wedged between my teeth
    from last nights flick,
a shakespeare for today.

where hamlet wears after-shave; endorses sportscars.

voice-over 1.5

I want now to write about beauty and the eternal reward
   - Julia Steele

two girls down the stretch of street, same shoes,
         thick platform, same hat, & clothes.

i have nothing to say to you now. to say now.

between letters, le   s, open a
         discourse into another headgear.

emotion betrays everything. tears on the
         heartfelt pillow. takes her

comfort there.

it is not a failing
to leave the word for luck out of recipe
  - Karen Houle, Ballast

the coffee stain becomes warm. leave out
      the words for snow, hail.

the left hand cannot be left. ever compared
      to the right hand, others.

or to have a hand in all of this.

once fell in love w/ a plumber. her hands
      were rough, could

break a boy like me in two.

mention is not to be mentioned
   - David UU

you my, you me, speak spark,
    answer nothing

epyllion condense, epitome
    marginalize in time

done, but w/ errors on the page

subsequent speech forgets

Well, who remembers a small purple and yellow bruise long?
  - Al Purdy, The Collected Poems

not every collect is a collection

not all select

tearing bits away the side

voice-over 2.0

for sue elmslie & wes folkieth

there is no limit to the galaxy's illusion.
  - *Robert Allen, The Assumption of Private Lives*

after reading playboy, or three pints
        of a campus homegrown

morcheeba, but more like
        a lion

grading out the years worth, signal hill
        to delaware

out to marine life, 1970, or the word,
        bookstore

rarely speaks so much

**You are yet far: far, for the water
too can be said to stretch distances**
   - *Angela Carr, Hero and Leander*

a profile of the visceral map: wherever i go
               for coffee comes a postcard.

to go & (   ) yr dog. my pretty.

two months of turkey, despite it all,
the modern greek woman
    can still be loved.

or ducking heads in scottish castles,
tess of montreal returning back

               to seasons of shade: deliberate,

after heat rings of the mediterranean;

sundogs, eyes.

The shock was a portal like this tiny black period.
   - *Senja Kunelius*

made flesh, or of something. ink,
    & the small scar left

behind the knee. the dagger
    draws me.

write fragments. not full sentences.
- Jon Paul Fiorentino

what makes, in a city. hill
& cross. upon said mark. mount.

(   ) is the perfect place
to look at the (   ).

i make no pretense
into (   ). oblivion.

**i write this note in newsprint
torn from the nests of rats and birds.**
- *Karen I. Press*

there is no such thing as the singular text.

i go to one city & then, even small towns
have some overwhelming going for.

a book by its cover: no dice. or whether
      the stitching is staple or glue.

its not the page count, but what
      you do w/ it. what matters.

& all the ghosts on the highway come hungry.

**and all this time his wife leaning against the counter
like she's got all day, keeping watch from a distance -**
- Aurian Haller

the push of where the bicycle, up hill eternal.

thank god its _____. weekly pressure
to hate the workweek. even so.

daughter takes to fireworks
& melts. loves it ever more.

crowds pressure up against the bar
& parliament. so tall, cant even

see the edge. bleeding speaker notes,
out into the far slopes going.

**For three years the pale knees of heaven
and the cave brilliant with amandines
his hand under her breast**
   - Natalee Caple

soot & other refuse scattered the black floor.

marking up mid-leg, on yr feet,
or on yr knees, live or die.

i had a problem w/ turning left
but only for two days. montreal
            or bust.

& take up an explanation of walking.

a whole half hour to get five minutes.

where field yields to town / a house folds into itself
   - jwcurry

how all becomes to misinterpret.
deliberate markers in place. arrows
            in.

greyhound bus by car. there, ive
            done it again.

it hurts to be (   ) all the time.
it hurts (to be).

& there people love in some places.
& there people live in some places.

two blocks away,
an acre folds in on itself. folds in.

time & time again. unyields.

names & other questions become apparent
   - *rob mclennan, paper hotel*

there are curves & learning & then there are
                 _____ _____. arch
         out a bit of back.

domination succeeds where apathy fails.
id burn the whole building down
           if i could.

its the nature of the nurture. games.

i have trouble reading into things.

(

) look out! (

)

between the lines.

I came here and you were not ready to speak
- Lisa Samuels

   notes: toward an explanation

1. dont trust language.

2. not every story has
    a) an ending.
    b) a purpose.

3. summer twitch & winter trail.

4. this is not what im supposed
    to be doing.

5.

extinct territory

invisible techniques (after gb

            the prairies have become
extinct territory, thats
what my heart says

            cant help, still get
that ticklish thrill
when i think of her,
                    open
                another email file

            & letters that pile up all
on this end, some ive written,
some ive only read

                completely see thru

summer: 31st year

i threw my hands in, swirl
of the sunny terrasse, are
    & then wondering, you in town?

bites down hard on my lip, she, quarters
& others that keep me holed,
    pigeon, sparrow, quail.

sleeps in the morning of small shadows,
opens her hair up to the shower rail
    & picturesque, wholly sweet.

this is the door i will design to open. this is
the bicycle that will take me. this
    is the key i will break.

light, darker, darkest, bright

~~take where the light flickers. over the hills~~

the light opens up & the fly goes
thru it. the fly goes thru
& burns, upon entry & re:
the light bulb. attractions
& the death of fire. icarus
abounds w/ wax, but no one
remembers the name

of his father, the half
who lived. who knew.
the difference. stories
of light & dark. or into
the sun. burning w/ cold,
the dark side

of the moon. in all these years,
she never could tell. a heat

like us.

heartbreak & the minds ugly furniture
- for donato mancini

a change is as good as
a charge

speculating on the point
& bookshelves moved

to the north wall

im not saying anything new
its just

my turn

defining locus
as where i am now

w/ bankbooks, coffee, loss
of the sense of magic, the minds
alchemical state

& source materials intact

old rocker new from apartment
my gran no longer needs

to get close to

diana, in hospital (morphine & demerol

the white knife turns, xrays show
leopard spots on bone

delerium & dreams creep, stone hearth
at 45, a vision

to know these windows well, foliage
& cards jungle city view

& absense of clocks, the pass of time
but lost to visits, dreary haze

encroaching truths, & clouds peer thru
dim clarity, tho rarely overwhelm

not once, even as the dose decreases
, wavers a bit

meanwhile (for bp

a.

bird flies off in one direction & then.
takes the rider off the
horse. off. takes.

rides a wave thru the top
& over. waves. learns.

a picture drawn. a thousand
words minus one.

b.

fore the insistance of trees. takes
a cornerstone of truth. &
shrubbery. toil.

enclave of rock.

c.

spot run. spot. dick & jane.
to save timmy, whos fallen down the well.
not lassie. not

spot. & then.
insistance, all. at the
same time. if.

only had eyes.

d.

vour & drink. out. dee-
light. or dark. the musicality

of leaves. left
the light on in the porch.

e.

raging, motion. munching
& crunching. at the.

concurrent. same. what.

f.

hands on. finger foods. perspective
divided by halves. at.

under the sun. same. she.
& aint no flies on me.

g.

netics. g. asterick.
asterix. little gaul. form

of ula. the certain pot.
or cauldron. g plus he.

or me. turns over. spoons.

h.

an h. a nayche. anne
heche. ant ache. an take.

aunt hayche. grass
hopper.

i.

or me. as the case may be.
or maybe. me, myself.

which is not. you. unless.
you are the one speaking. when

you becomes i. i, who is me.
or three. if not one,

or you. me, two.

j.

bird. on the quick. solar
or speaking out of turn.

across the street, or
between lights. work.

during the day he. pains.
skies over.

k.

mary. netics.
& metrics. com.

blues out. tear.
the roses. m.

becomes a. becomes
predominant letter.

before er. his
or hers. truly.

madly.

l.

sings a song of. lemon,
lake. swims to the bottom.

epistemic slide. relates.
or re-lates. to. too.

m.

take two, & two
thousand years.

add then, candy
coated chocolate.

m in your m. not
your hands.

n.

unaccepting nihalism.
no, no, no. oh.

grass the green way
of yellow bicycle. blew.

head lights yr eyes.
sun reflections

& the dead art.

o.

pen. makes
like a mouth.
shout. out.
& again. smoke.
rings in yr fingers.
throws. circles
& circumnavigate.
o. & then.
oh. owe.
like money. what

i give you. what
you must give back.

p.

bum jokes. cock
in her mouth.

releasing fluid. drunk out
at the side of the road.

or behind bushes. peter
peter. put her in

a pumpkin shell. & there he
kept her. part

of the circle length. a pi.

q.

where laughter
ensues. funniest

letter. but nothing
w/out u.

r.

ushes. abbits.
ansack the adishes.

a. a. a.

s.

permanent hillsides, making
snakes in the grass.

twirls around something
like it doesnt know its shape.

sings for meals & lodgings.
supper, sleep. the high note

catching.

t.

boston parties,
wont go there again.

no sugar tonight. line
in a perfect cross.

the line fit
to a t. love,

leave.

u.

resembling nothing.
two hands in a cup.

gathering water, sand.
a bucket of stones.

grain dust
feeds the fish.

v.

water marks. or
making a point. or into.

birds fly over
cartoon fields. a sun.

o v,
u.   light rays penetrating,

pinpricks in the heart.

w.

buffalo railroad,
two qs. thanks.

your welcome. where.
& four more at the end.

x.

spots. marks.
points on a grid.

two os or three.
a tic, a tac, a toe.

alone. decides.
insistance in the favour.

presenting tuppence,
& contract to the name.

& dotted line, unbroken.

y.

oh why oh why.
because because.

answer a question
w/ a question. dont tell.

gets beyond me. tell well.
h e double hockey sticks.

z.

a, b, c & 1, 2, 3.
or wed, bed, dead.

doesnt matter. one north,
one south. we both think

were rite. right.

The author of seven previous poetry collections, rob mclennan has published poetry, fiction & critical writing in Canada, the US, India, the Czech Republic, Ireland, England & Australia. The editor/publisher of above/ground press & the longpoem magazine STANZAS, he edits the cauldron books series through Broken Jaw Press, & most recently, the anthologies side/lines: a new canadian poetics (Insomniac Press) & GROUNDSWELL: the best of above/ground press, 1993-2003 (cauldron books #4, Broken Jaw Press). A resident of Glengarry County, Ontario, he currently lives in Ottawa, where he co-ordinates events & the semi-annual ottawa small press book fair through the small press action network - ottawa (span-o). He is completing a novel, a collection of essays, & a poetry ms, the news. With Ottawa poet Stephen Brockwell, he recently launched Poetics.ca, & can be reached via www.track0.com/rob_mclennan

red earth
7

voice-over 1.0
31

voice-over 1.5
51

96

voice-over 2.0
59

extinct territory
73

meanwhile
81